THE GREAT RECESSION

The Shocking Truth about the
2008 Financial Crisis

Prabal Jain

Riverwood Capital

Riverwood Capital®

CONTENTS

INTRODUCTION

As the excesses and unchecked ambitions of the financial sector continued to escalate, the consequences became increasingly evident. It was a period marked by massive private gains and a grievous public loss. The belief that one could conjure something out of nothing had taken hold, and resistance to this allure proved challenging.

The financial industry had, in many ways, turned into a high-stakes game with catastrophic consequences for the public. Massive private gains were being enjoyed at the expense of the wider population. The recklessness and disregard for the repercussions of these actions were clear indicators of a system teetering on the brink of disaster.

Amid the unfolding crisis, there was a concerning sentiment among some—a desire to return to the old ways of operating, to revert to the practices that had precipitated the crisis in the first place. This inclination, driven by the allure of quick gains and financial excess, posed a significant threat to the prospects of lasting reform.

Whistleblowers and Concerned Voices

In the midst of this tumultuous period, anonymous emails from within the banking industry began to surface. Bankers, wary of repercussions, expressed their deep concerns about the unfolding crisis. Their messages were a glimpse into the anxieties that pervaded the industry's ranks, highlighting the depth of the crisis.

The crisis also laid bare the shortcomings of regulatory bodies. Despite having the power to intervene and enforce regulations, regulators often hesitated to take action. This failure to act allowed many of the practices that contributed to the crisis to continue unchecked.

The Global Fallout

In September 2008, Lehman Brothers' bankruptcy and the collapse of AIG triggered a global financial crisis of unprecedented scale. Stock markets worldwide tumbled, and the global economy plunged into recession. The aftermath was catastrophic, costing the world tens of trillions of dollars, rendering millions unemployed, and doubling the national debt of the United States.

The 2008 crisis was not an isolated incident but part of a pattern that had emerged since the 1980s. The rise of the U.S. financial sector had ushered in a series of increasingly severe financial crises. Each crisis caused more significant damage while the industry continued to amass wealth.

CHAPTER 1: THE ERA OF DEREGULATION

In the aftermath of the Great Depression, the United States embarked on a remarkable era of economic growth that spanned four decades, remarkably free from the specter of financial crises. This period of stability was rooted in a tightly regulated financial industry, where most banks operated as local businesses, and speculative activities were strictly curtailed.

The regulatory framework that emerged after the Great Depression placed stringent controls on the financial sector. Regular banks, the backbone of local communities, were prohibited from engaging in speculative activities. These institutions were trusted with safeguarding the savings of everyday citizens, and regulations ensured that they did not take undue risks with those funds.

Investment Banking in the Traditional Model

Investment banks of this era operated on a traditional partnership model. In this model, the partners had a personal stake in the success of the firm. They put their own capital at risk, fostering a culture of prudence and careful financial stewardship. The partners were motivated to generate profits but were equally cautious about protecting their investments.

Paul Volcker played a pivotal role in shaping the financial landscape during this period. He served in the Treasury Department and later became the Chairman of the Federal

Reserve from 1979 to 1987. Before entering government service, Volcker was a financial economist at Chase Manhattan Bank. His experiences provided him with valuable insights into the financial sector.

The Explosive Growth of the 1980s

However, as the 1980s dawned, a seismic shift began to take place in the financial industry. The regulatory constraints that had maintained stability for decades began to erode. Investment banks, once conservative and privately held partnerships, started to go public, resulting in an infusion of substantial capital.

This transformation of investment banks had far-reaching consequences. It allowed them to amass significant financial resources and expand their operations on a global scale. What was once a small, traditional investment bank like Morgan Stanley had grown into a financial behemoth with tens of thousands of employees and offices worldwide.

The shift towards deregulation and the proliferation of financial conglomerates marked a significant turning point in the financial industry's history. The balance between risk and responsibility was shifting, and the consequences of this shift would reverberate far into the future.

The Dawn of Financial Deregulation

The 1980s ushered in a period of unprecedented transformation in the financial industry. Investment banks, which were once small and conservative partnerships, exploded in size and scope. Morgan Stanley, which once had only 110 personnel and a single office with $12 million in capital, had become a financial juggernaut with tens of thousands of employees, offices around the world, and billions in capital. This expansion coincided with the era of financial deregulation, an era that would reshape the industry and the fortunes of those on Wall Street.

The investment banks' decision to go public had profound consequences. They gained access to vast amounts of stockholder money, which fueled their growth and global expansion. The people on Wall Street began accumulating wealth at an astonishing rate. The transformation was striking—individuals who once had to supplement their incomes with night jobs were now earning millions of dollars, attributing their success to their perceived intelligence.

Reaganomics and Financial Deregulation

In 1981, President Ronald Reagan selected Donald Regan, the CEO of Merrill Lynch, as the Secretary of the Treasury. This choice signaled a close alignment between Wall Street and the Reagan administration. Many Wall Street leaders strongly supported the president's economic policies. Under the Reagan administration, with the backing of economists and financial lobbyists, the United States embarked on a 30-year period of financial deregulation.

One of the early signs of the consequences of deregulation emerged in 1982 when the Reagan administration deregulated Savings and Loan (S&L) companies, allowing them to engage in risky investments with their depositors' money. By the end of the decade, hundreds of S&Ls had failed, costing taxpayers a staggering $124 billion and causing countless individuals to lose their life savings. This period was marked by one of the most significant bank heists in American history.

The Rise of Alan Greenspan

The story of Charles Keating, his association with economist Alan Greenspan, and the subsequent consequences serves as a critical backdrop to the era of financial deregulation. After Federal

Regulators began investigating Keating in 1985, he sought the counsel of Alan Greenspan. In a letter addressed to regulators, Greenspan vouched for Keating's business acumen, endorsing his sound business plans and expertise. Shockingly, Greenspan saw no risk in allowing Keating to invest his customers' money, and he was reportedly compensated with $40,000 for his services. However, Keating's legal troubles didn't end there, and he would soon find himself in prison.

Meanwhile, Alan Greenspan's career continued to ascend. President Reagan appointed him as the Chairman of America's Central Bank, the Federal Reserve. Greenspan's tenure at the Federal Reserve was marked by a remarkable degree of continuity, as he was reappointed by Presidents Clinton and George W. Bush. However, his stewardship of the Federal Reserve would have far-reaching implications for the financial industry and the broader economy.

During the Clinton administration, the momentum of financial deregulation persisted. Key figures like Treasury Secretaries Robert Rubin, a former CEO of the investment bank Goldman Sachs, and Larry Summers, a Harvard economics professor, played pivotal roles in shaping policy. The financial sector, characterized by its power, influential lobbying efforts, and vast financial resources, gradually captured the political system. This influence extended to both Democratic and Republican political circles.

The Consolidation of Financial Giants

By the late 1990s, the financial sector had undergone a significant transformation. It had consolidated into a few gigantic firms, each of them so substantial that their potential failure could threaten the entire financial system. The Clinton administration facilitated the growth of these behemoths. In 1998, Citicorp and Travelers merged to form Citigroup, which became the largest financial services company globally. This merger, however, violated the

Glass-Steagall Act, a Depression-era law designed to prevent banks with consumer deposits from engaging in risky investment banking activities.

Remarkably, the Federal Reserve, under Greenspan's leadership, remained largely silent about this violation for a year. Then, with the encouragement of figures like Larry Summers and Robert Rubin, the law was ultimately repealed in 1999. The repeal of the Glass-Steagall Act marked a pivotal moment in financial history, allowing banks to engage more freely in risky investment activities.

In the chapters ahead, we will continue to explore the consequences of this era of continued deregulation, tracing the path to the financial crisis of 2008. We will examine how the consolidation of financial giants and the relaxation of regulations set the stage for the events that would ultimately lead to one of the most devastating financial crises in modern history.

CHAPTER 2: THE ERA
OF MEGA-BANKS

The repeal of the Glass-Steagall Act in 1999 through the Gramm-Leach-Bliley Act, often known as the Citigroup Relief Act, marked a pivotal moment in financial history. The Glass-Steagall Act had been a critical safeguard, preventing banks with consumer deposits from engaging in risky investment banking activities. With the removal of this regulatory barrier, the path was cleared for future mergers and the ascent of mega-banks.

Why do we have big banks? The answer is multifaceted. Banks crave the monopoly of power, they thrive on lobbying influence, and they understand that when they become too big, they will be considered "too big to fail." Mega-banks wield immense market power, enabling them to shape financial landscapes to their advantage.

However, financial markets are inherently unstable, or at least potentially so. An apt metaphor is an oil tanker – they are enormous vessels, requiring compartments to prevent the sloshing of oil from capsizing the ship. Regulations, introduced during the aftermath of the Great Depression, established these watertight compartments. Deregulation, on the other hand, dismantled the safeguards, effectively ending the compartmentalization that had provided stability.

The late 1990s saw investment banks fueling a massive bubble in internet stocks. This speculative frenzy was characterized by irrational exuberance, with investors pouring billions into tech companies with sky-high valuations. However, in 2001, the bubble burst, leading to a crash that resulted in a staggering five trillion dollars in investment losses.

The Securities and Exchange Commission (SEC), a federal agency created during the Depression to regulate investment banking, failed to take meaningful action during this period. Despite the glaring risks and excesses, regulatory bodies largely remained passive. Given the evident failure of self-regulation, external interventions became necessary.

Elliott Spitzer's investigation shed light on the practices of investment banks during this tumultuous period. It revealed that investment banks had promoted internet companies they knew would fail. Stock analysts, motivated by the business they brought in, often provided public statements that contradicted their private assessments.

The Analyst Scandal And Regulatory Responses

The revelations of the analyst scandal sent shockwaves through the financial industry. Investment banks had promoted internet companies they knew were destined to fail. Stock analysts, whose opinions held great influence, were incentivized based on the business they brought in, leading to stark disparities between their public pronouncements and private assessments.

Infospace, once given the highest possible rating, was dismissed by an analyst as a piece of junk. Similarly, Excite, also highly rated, was disparaged as a "piece of crap." The pervasive practice of misleading investors was not an isolated occurrence; it was systemic. The belief that "everybody's doing it" prevailed, eroding trust in the integrity of analysts' recommendations.

In December 2002, ten investment banks settled the case for

a total of $1.4 billion and pledged to reform their practices. This landmark settlement marked a turning point and a tacit admission of wrongdoing within the industry.

Scott Talbot, the chief lobbyist for the Financial Services Roundtable, a powerful group in Washington representing nearly all of the world's largest financial companies, was pressed on the matter. The question posed was whether he was comfortable with the fact that several of the member companies had engaged in large-scale criminal activity. The response was evasive, highlighting the influence and complexities surrounding lobbying efforts.

However, specific instances of criminal activity within financial institutions were not limited to the analyst scandal. Citibank, for instance, was found to have assisted in funneling $100 million of drug money out of Mexico, leading to questions about accountability. The response to such allegations was sometimes dismissive, raising concerns about the culture within financial institutions.

Between 1998 and 2003, Fannie Mae faced its own set of challenges. The institution, originally created to support home financing, encountered difficulties and controversies that would have far-reaching implications for the housing market and the broader economy.

We will continue to explore the repercussions of these scandals and regulatory responses. We will examine how the financial industry grappled with a loss of trust and integrity and how these challenges set the stage for the events leading up to the 2008 financial crisis. This is a story of accountability, ethics, and the complex relationship between financial institutions and the regulatory framework that governs them.

CHAPTER 3: FINANCIAL SCANDALS AND THE COMPLEXITY OF DERIVATIVES

As the financial industry grappled with a loss of trust and the aftermath of scandals like the analyst scandal, new controversies emerged. Citibank's involvement in facilitating the flow of drug money out of Mexico raised eyebrows, but responses ranged from dismissive to evasive.

Fannie Mae's Overstatement

Between 1998 and 2003, Fannie Mae faced its own set of challenges. The institution, initially created to support home financing, came under scrutiny for overstating its earnings by over $10 billion. Navigating the complex landscape of accounting standards, which often require determinations over which experts frequently disagree, proved to be a daunting task. CEO Franklin Raines, who previously served as President Clinton's budget director, received over $52 million in bonuses during this period.

When UBS was caught assisting wealthy Americans in evading taxes, they chose not to cooperate with the U.S. government. The issue of cooperation and the complexities surrounding treaty frameworks became a point of contention. Despite the magnitude of the fines imposed on such companies, they often did not have to admit any wrongdoing.

The financial services industry seemed to exhibit a level of criminality that set it apart. This observation prompted questions about why high-tech companies like Cisco, Intel, Google, Apple, and IBM didn't face similar issues. High-tech industries, inherently creative, derive their value from innovation and creation, which contrasted starkly with the financial sector's troubles.

The Rise of Derivatives and the Battle for Regulation

The 1990s witnessed a seismic shift in the financial landscape. Deregulation and technological advancements gave birth to a proliferation of complex financial products known as derivatives. While economists and bankers contended that these instruments would enhance market safety, the outcome was strikingly different – they introduced instability.

As the Cold War ended, many former physicists and mathematicians redirected their skills from Cold War technology to financial markets. They collaborated with investment bankers, devising financial instruments that were, in the words of Warren Buffett, akin to "weapons of mass destruction." Regulators, politicians, and business leaders initially underestimated the potential threat of financial innovation to the stability of the financial system.

Derivatives allowed bankers to gamble on a multitude of factors, from the rise or fall of oil prices to the bankruptcy of a company and even the weather. By the late 1990s, the derivatives market had ballooned into a $50 trillion unregulated behemoth.

In 1998, Brooksley Born, a distinguished legal scholar who had chaired the Commodity Futures Trading Commission (CFTC), recognized the gravity of the situation. The CFTC, tasked with overseeing the derivatives market, proposed regulations to address the growing concerns. However, the response from

Clinton's Treasury Department was swift and vehement.

Larry Summers, then part of the Treasury Department, made a forceful intervention, directing Born to halt her efforts to regulate derivatives. The major banks relied heavily on these activities for their earnings, setting the stage for a fierce and protracted battle. Summers, representing the interests of the financial sector, clashed with regulators like Brooksley Born, who were deeply concerned about the risks posed by unbridled derivatives trading.

The Derivatives Battle and Unregulated Markets

As Brooksley Born, then Chair of the Commodity Futures Trading Commission (CFTC), attempted to regulate derivatives, she encountered fierce resistance. Larry Summers, representing the interests of major banks, brought 13 bankers into his office, pressuring Born to cease her regulatory efforts. These banks heavily relied on derivative activities for their earnings, setting the stage for a monumental battle.

Following the call from Summers, Alan Greenspan, Robert Rubin, and SEC Chairman Arthur Levitt issued a joint statement. In it, they condemned Born's efforts and recommended legislation to maintain the unregulated status of derivatives. This statement laid the groundwork for a legislative response.

In 2000, Senator Phil Gramm played a significant role in the passage of a bill that essentially exempted derivatives from regulation. The Commodity Futures Modernization Act, crafted with the assistance of financial industry lobbyists, was enacted. It effectively banned the regulation of derivatives, paving the way for their unchecked proliferation.

With the regulatory barriers lifted, the use of derivatives and financial innovation surged dramatically after 2000. The financial industry embraced these instruments, and unregulated markets flourished. By the time George W. Bush assumed the presidency in 2001, the U.S. financial industry was operating in an environment of limited oversight and unprecedented financial innovation.

In the forthcoming chapters, we will delve into the consequences of this unregulated landscape. We will explore how the explosive growth of derivatives and financial innovation set the stage for a financial system that was increasingly complex and prone to instability. This is a story of regulatory choices and their far-reaching impacts on the financial industry and the global economy.

CHAPTER 4: THE UNREGULATED FINANCIAL FRONTIER

As George W. Bush took office in 2001, the U.S. financial industry found itself navigating uncharted territory. The legislative success of the Commodity Futures Modernization Act in 2000 had effectively exempted derivatives from regulation. This deregulatory shift allowed for the unrestrained expansion of financial innovation and the proliferation of complex financial instruments.

With the regulatory shackles removed, the financial sector embraced the newfound freedom to develop and trade an array of intricate financial products. These innovations ranged from exotic derivatives to complex structured financial instruments. The industry found itself in a golden era of financial experimentation.

Financial innovation, driven by the pursuit of profit and sophistication, introduced a level of complexity previously unseen in the market. These innovations often obscured the true nature of financial instruments, making it challenging for even seasoned professionals to fully understand their risks.

One of the significant developments during this period was the rise of securitization. Financial institutions bundled various types of loans, from mortgages to credit card debt, into securities that were then sold to investors. These securities, often backed by the cash flows generated from the underlying loans, became increasingly complex and opaque.

Credit rating agencies played a pivotal role in this environment, assigning ratings to these securities. These ratings were meant to provide investors with guidance on the risk associated with the securities. However, they often failed to accurately assess the risks, contributing to a false sense of security among investors.

The complexity of these financial innovations had global implications. As these instruments were traded internationally, interconnectedness within the global financial system grew, making it susceptible to systemic risks.

The Mortgage Meltdown and Predatory Lending

The financial landscape was evolving rapidly, with one of the most significant developments being the popularity of Collateralized Debt Obligations (CDOs). These financial instruments gained favor with retirement funds, which were restricted to purchasing highly-rated securities. However, this seemingly profitable system was concealing a ticking time bomb.

Lenders, under the shadow of a flawed system, grew increasingly reckless in their lending practices. They cared little about the borrower's ability to repay and instead focused on making riskier loans. The investment banks, orchestrators of the CDO market, were equally unconcerned about the quality of the underlying mortgages. Selling more CDOs translated to higher profits, creating a dangerous incentive structure.

Compounding the problem, rating agencies, whose income depended on fees from investment banks, faced no liability if their CDO ratings proved erroneous. This lack of accountability gave a green light to the proliferation of risky financial products.

The Subprime Boom

Between 2000 and 2003, the number of mortgage loans issued each year nearly quadrupled. The securitization process focused on volume rather than the quality of mortgages. Risky subprime loans surged in popularity during this time. Yet, many of these subprime loans, when bundled into CDOs, still received AAA ratings.

In hindsight, there were opportunities to create derivative products with safeguards, limiting the risks involved. However, these measures were not implemented. This lack of foresight and precaution would prove costly.

The financial institutions' incentives were heavily skewed toward selling the most profitable products, which often meant pushing predatory loans. Mortgage brokers, driven by the promise of higher commissions, directed borrowers towards subprime loans, fully aware of the risks involved.

In the upcoming chapters, we will continue to explore the consequences of these lending practices and the systemic risks they posed. This is a story of risky financial products, flawed incentives, and the growing imbalance in the mortgage market.

CHAPTER 5: THE HOUSING BUBBLE AND THE FINANCIAL FRENZY

Between 2001 and 2007, the financial landscape experienced a whirlwind of activity, fueled by the surging flow of hundreds of billions of dollars through the securitization chain. This era saw the emergence of the largest financial bubble in history, driven primarily by the real estate market.

The Housing Frenzy

The housing market experienced an unprecedented boom. Home purchases and housing prices soared to dizzying heights. However, the rapid rise in housing prices appeared irrational, driven by a financing frenzy within the financial sector. The allure of homeownership was a potent driver. Real estate represented tangible assets that individuals could see, live in, or rent out. This perception created a speculative fervor that defied economic sense.

The financial sector played a pivotal role in this housing bubble. Its appetite for financing, combined with a herd mentality, influenced the decisions of many. This mirrored the late 1980s housing bubble, but this time, the stakes were much higher. Financial institutions such as Goldman Sachs, Bear Stearns, Lehman Brothers, and Merrill Lynch were deeply entrenched in this frenzy. The subprime lending market, in particular, witnessed explosive growth, increasing from $30 billion to over $600 billion in a decade. The profits generated were astronomical, as exemplified by Countrywide Financial's $11 billion in profits.

On Wall Street, annual cash bonuses skyrocketed, turning traders and CEOs into billionaires. For instance, Lehman Brothers, a top underwriter of subprime lending, paid its CEO Richard Fuld a staggering $485 million. A significant portion of the profits generated during this period was illusory. It was money created by the system and booked as income, even though it was built on a shaky foundation. The housing bubble resembled a massive national and global Ponzi scheme.

Despite the growing frenzy, regulatory authorities had to regulate the mortgage industry under the Home Ownership and Equity Protection Act. However, their actions, or lack thereof, would have profound consequences for the financial industry and the economy.

Regulatory Inaction and the Leverage Dilemma

In the lead-up to the financial crisis, regulatory oversight and the management of leverage were critical factors that could have influenced the trajectory of the impending crisis. However, the decisions made—or not made—by key figures in the financial world had far-reaching consequences.

Under the Home Ownership and Equity Protection Act, the Federal Reserve Board had to regulate the mortgage industry. However, Federal Reserve Chairman Alan Greenspan remained steadfast in his refusal to utilize this authority. Greenspan's ideological opposition to regulation hindered any meaningful action.

Consumer advocacy groups, such as Greenlining, recognized the complexity and opacity of mortgage instruments like those offered by Countrywide. They provided evidence of the need for regulatory intervention, hoping to sway Greenspan's stance. However, their efforts proved fruitless, as Greenspan remained committed to his ideology.

Over time, regulatory agencies like the SEC saw a decline in their capacity to effectively oversee financial markets. The enforcement division of the SEC was reduced, and the SEC's office of risk management operated with just one staff member, hampering its ability to identify and mitigate risks.

As the housing bubble inflated, investment banks sought to maximize their profits by borrowing heavily to acquire more loans and create more Collateralized Debt Obligations (CDOs). This strategy introduced a critical element: leverage. The ratio between borrowed money and the banks' own capital was a crucial indicator of the industry's vulnerability.

The ever-increasing leverage posed a significant systemic risk. Despite the apparent danger, the allure of short-term profits clouded the judgment of many financial institutions. This insatiable appetite for leverage would play a pivotal role in the impending financial crisis.

CHAPTER 6: THE DANGEROUS LEVERAGE AND THE AIG TIME BOMB

As the housing bubble swelled, investment banks were on a borrowing spree, heavily leveraging their positions to fuel their insatiable appetite for mortgage loans and the creation of Collateralized Debt Obligations (CDOs). Leverage, the ratio between borrowed money and a bank's own capital, became a key indicator of the industry's vulnerability.

With each passing day, investment banks increased their leverage. The more they borrowed, the higher their leverage ratio soared. This dangerous practice left them highly exposed to even minor fluctuations in asset values.

In 2004, Henry Paulson, the CEO of Goldman Sachs, played a pivotal role in lobbying the Securities and Exchange Commission (SEC) to relax limits on leverage. This regulatory change allowed banks to significantly escalate their borrowing, a move that defied common sense.

The SEC's decision to permit investment banks to take on more leverage was met with bewilderment. It seemed an inexplicable move given the potential risks it posed. The decision would have far-reaching consequences that would soon become evident.

Despite concerns about the rising levels of leverage, the SEC proceeded with the rule changes. Commissioners voted unanimously to adopt the new rules, effectively giving investment banks the green light to amplify their borrowing.

The financial system was now operating at an alarming level of leverage. Investment banks were leveraged as high as 33 to 1, which meant that even a tiny 3% decrease in asset values could push them to the brink of collapse.

AIG and Credit Default Swaps

While the investment banks were diving into the abyss of leverage, another ticking time bomb lurked in the financial system: AIG, the world's largest insurance company. AIG had been peddling massive quantities of derivatives known as credit default swaps (CDS), which would play a pivotal role in the impending financial crisis.

Credit default swaps were essentially insurance contracts. Investors who owned CDOs could purchase CDS from AIG by paying a quarterly premium. In return, AIG promised to compensate these investors for any losses they incurred if the CDOs turned sour. However, the unique aspect of CDS was that speculators could also buy them from AIG to bet against CDOs they didn't even own. This key distinction from traditional insurance allowed multiple parties to insure the same asset.

Unlike conventional insurance, credit default swaps were largely unregulated. AIG was not required to set aside any reserves to cover potential losses, a stark contrast to the stringent financial safeguards demanded of traditional insurers. Instead, AIG rewarded its employees with hefty cash bonuses as soon as these CDS contracts were signed. However, if the CDOs backing these contracts went belly up, AIG would be left holding the bag.

AIG's employees were essentially incentivized to take colossal risks during the good times to generate short-term revenue and profits, which translated into substantial bonuses. This distorted compensation system disregarded the long-term consequences it could unleash and paved the way for the firm's eventual financial downfall.

AIG's Risky Business - The Warning Signs

As AIG's Financial Products division dabbled in the perilous world of credit default swaps (CDS), an insidious system of compensation reared its head. The flawed incentive structure within the division, which rewarded massive risk-taking during the good times, had far-reaching consequences.

AIG's employees were lured into taking enormous risks with the promise of substantial short-term gains. The system of compensation prioritized immediate revenue and profits, resulting in hefty bonuses for employees. However, this model neglected the long-term implications of their actions and ultimately sowed the seeds of AIG's future financial ruin.

AIG's Financial Products division in London was at the epicenter of this risky behavior. They issued a staggering $500 billion worth of credit default swaps during the housing bubble, many of which were tied to CDOs backed by subprime mortgages. The division, comprising 400 employees, collectively raked in $3.5 billion in bonuses during the period from 2000 to 2007.

At the helm of AIGFP was Joseph Cassano, who personally reaped the rewards of this high-stakes game. He pocketed a staggering $315 million during this period. It seemed that within the realm of AIGFP, there was an unwavering belief that nothing could go wrong.

In 2007, AIG's auditors sounded the alarm, cautioning against the risks posed by their CDS transactions. Joseph St. Dennis, one of these auditors, went as far as resigning in frustration when his attempts to investigate AIGFP's accounting practices were repeatedly thwarted by Cassano.

CHAPTER 7: THE DEAF EARS OF THE FINANCIAL ELITE

Raghuram Rajan's Warning

In 2005, Raghuram Rajan, the Chief Economist of the International Monetary Fund (IMF), delivered a paper at the renowned Jackson Hole Symposium. This prestigious gathering included luminaries like Ben Bernanke, Larry Summers, Timothy Geithner, and Alan Greenspan. Rajan's paper posed a critical question: "Is financial development making the world riskier?"

Rajan's paper delved into the incentive structures prevailing in the financial world, structures that encouraged colossal cash bonuses predicated on short-term profits while imposing no penalties for future losses. He argued that these incentives were driving bankers to take increasingly risky actions, actions that could potentially undermine their own institutions and even the entire financial system.

Rajan underscored the importance of compensating individuals based on risk-adjusted performance. He contended that the prevailing system made it easy for financial institutions to enhance performance by assuming more risk. In essence, Rajan argued that these incentives were a ticking time bomb, hiding the potential consequences of their actions.

Rajan's paper struck a chord with some, but not all. Larry Summers, in particular, was vocal in his disagreement. Summers perceived Rajan's critique as an attack on the changing financial landscape and expressed concerns about potential regulations that could reverse this transformation. He accused Rajan of being a Luddite, fearing that excessive regulation might stifle the financial sector.

As the debate raged on, it became apparent that the lure of astronomical bonuses was driving some financial elites to overlook the inherent risks in their actions. The potential rewards, measured in millions or even tens of millions of dollars, overshadowed concerns about the systemic risks they were creating.

Despite Raghuram Rajan's prescient warnings and the voices of caution, the financial elite continued down a perilous path, one that would ultimately lead to a devastating global financial crisis.

CHAPTER 8: THE EXCESSES OF WALL STREET

Lavish Lifestyles and Risk-Taking Culture

Within the world of high finance, extravagance and excess had become the norm. Executives like Richard Fuld, the CEO of Lehman Brothers, epitomized this culture of opulence.

Richard Fuld's lifestyle was a testament to extreme wealth. He owned a $14 million oceanfront mansion in Florida, a summer vacation home in Sun Valley, Idaho, and an art collection filled with million-dollar paintings. His personal elevator was a symbol of his disconnection from the everyday reality of his employees and the financial risks his firm was taking.

Fuld's elevator was a well-guarded enclave, allowing him to avoid interaction with the very people whose livelihoods were tied to his decisions. The extravagance didn't stop there; Lehman Brothers owned a fleet of corporate jets, including two 767s, and even a helicopter.

The financial industry had become a realm of extreme risk-taking and competition. Bankers constantly pushed the envelope, engaging in increasingly larger deals, often exceeding $50 billion and even reaching $100 billion. The desire to outdo one another became a defining characteristic of this high-stakes environment.

The financial elite were known for their impulsive behaviors, both within and outside the workplace. These traits manifested in various ways, from risk-taking in their business dealings to extravagant lifestyles that included visits to strip clubs and recreational drug use.

Wall Street's Dark Underbelly - Vice and Excess

Beneath the facade of Wall Street's high-powered financial dealings lay a dark underbelly of vice and excessive behavior. The pursuit of wealth and success often led to reckless lifestyles and moral compromises.

Recent neuroscientific experiments shed light on the psychology of financial professionals. When exposed to the prospect of earning money, the same parts of the brain activated by cocaine were stimulated. This link between money and brain chemistry underscored the powerful allure of financial success. In the cutthroat world of finance, many believed that engaging in questionable behavior was necessary to climb the corporate ladder, gain recognition, and secure promotions. This mindset fostered a culture of indulgence and excess.

Business entertainment accounted for a significant portion of revenue for New York derivatives brokers, amounting to around five percent. These extravagances often included strip clubs, prostitution, and drug use. One lawsuit filed against a brokerage firm alleged that brokers were required to arrange for prostitutes to entertain traders. Some financial professionals had no qualms about misusing corporate funds for personal pleasures. Clients, often representing major Wall Street firms like Goldman Sachs, Lehman Brothers, and Morgan Stanley, indulged in lavish and inappropriate expenses, including expensive cars and entertainment.

This pattern of behavior was not confined to junior employees; it extended to senior management as well. Senior executives were equally complicit in engaging in questionable practices, demonstrating a pervasive culture of excess throughout the industry.

The moral erosion within the financial sector not only had personal consequences but also raised questions about the industry's values and ethics. As the pursuit of profit took precedence, the boundaries between right and wrong blurred, contributing to the volatile atmosphere that would eventually lead to the financial crisis.

CHAPTER 9: THE SUBPRIME MORTGAGE DISASTER

The subprime mortgage disaster unfolded as a stark example of reckless lending practices and financial negligence. delves into the dangerous world of subprime mortgages, where borrowers had little to no equity in their homes, setting the stage for a catastrophic financial crisis.

Subprime mortgages were a risky business. Borrowers often put down minimal or no money for their homes, leaving them with little financial stake in the property. If anything went wrong, they had little incentive to continue making payments, making these loans a high-stakes gamble. Goldman Sachs, a prominent player in the financial industry, was deeply involved in the subprime mortgage market. They packaged and sold subprime mortgages in the form of complex collateralized debt obligations (CDOs). These CDOs, despite their inherent risk, were often rated as safe as government securities by rating agencies.

Betting Against the Market

In late 2006, as the subprime mortgage crisis deepened, Goldman Sachs took an audacious step. They didn't just sell toxic CDOs; they actively started betting against them, essentially wagering on their failure while assuring customers of their high quality. uncovers this high-stakes game and its far-reaching implications.

Henry Paulson, the former CEO of Goldman Sachs, made

a remarkable transition from the financial industry to the government. He accepted the role of Secretary of the Treasury under President George W. Bush. Despite his substantial financial sacrifices, this move proved to be a lucrative decision, thanks to a tax law that saved him $50 million in taxes on the $485 million of Goldman stock he had to sell.

One of the casualties of the subprime mortgage crisis was the public employees' retirement system of Mississippi. This institution, responsible for the financial well-being of over 80,000 retirees, lost millions of dollars due to investments in now-worthless securities. They have taken legal action against Goldman Sachs.

Goldman Sachs went further than merely selling toxic CDOs; they began betting against them by purchasing credit default swaps from AIG. This strategy allowed Goldman to profit when the CDOs they sold to others failed. While this was happening, they continued to assure their customers that these securities were top-quality investments.

Goldman Sachs's massive exposure to AIG's credit default swaps meant they were deeply concerned about AIG's solvency. To protect themselves, they spent $150 million to purchase insurance on their own exposure to AIG, in case AIG went bankrupt.

The Dark Side of Sales

Goldman Sachs faced severe criticism for selling $600 million worth of Timberwolf Securities, despite internal emails from employees expressing concerns about the quality of the product. These emails, referring to Timberwolf as a "shitty deal" and "crap," raised ethical questions about the responsibility of financial institutions to their clients.

The discussion centers on the fiduciary duty of financial institutions to act in the best interests of their clients. Questions were raised about whether Goldman Sachs properly disclosed its adverse interests when selling securities that its own employees deemed problematic.

CHAPTER 10: IGNORING THE WARNING SIGNS

The Federal Reserve and its leaders, including Ben Bernanke, downplayed the possibility of a housing bubble and the risks associated with subprime lending. Ben Bernanke, who became chairman of the Federal Reserve Board in February 2006, dismissed concerns about a housing bubble and a potential recession, calling it a "pretty unlikely possibility." He stated that there had never been a nationwide decline in house prices.

Despite multiple warnings and meetings with experts like Robert Gnaizda, who expressed concerns about the housing market, the Federal Reserve took little action in the years leading up to the crisis. Frederick Mishkin, one of the Federal Reserve board Governors under Bernanke's leadership, faced criticism for downplaying the risks of the housing market in his academic research. This raised questions about the objectivity and credibility of Federal Reserve officials. It wasn't until 2009 that Bernanke and the Federal Reserve board began to acknowledge the severity of the housing crisis. This acknowledgment came after years of warnings from experts and the rapid deterioration of the housing market.

As early as 2004, the FBI had begun to issue warnings about a growing epidemic of mortgage fraud. These warnings included concerns about inflated appraisals and fraudulent loan documentation, highlighting the fraudulent activity that was rampant within the mortgage industry.

In 2005, the IMF's Chief Economist, Raghuram Rajan, sounded the alarm about the dangerous incentives within the financial system that could lead to a crisis. His warnings emphasized the need for caution and oversight.

In 2006, economist Nouriel Roubini gained attention for his predictions about the impending collapse of the housing bubble and the subsequent financial crisis. His analyses and warnings were seen as prescient.

In 2007, journalist Alan Sloan published articles in Fortune Magazine and The Washington Post, drawing attention to the issues within the housing and financial markets. His reporting added to the growing chorus of voices expressing concern.

The International Monetary Fund (IMF) repeatedly issued warnings about the impending crisis, emphasizing its severity and potential global impact.

Expert Warnings Go Unheeded

Despite the mounting warnings from various experts and institutions, including hedge fund manager Bill Ackman and author Charles Morris, many key players in the financial industry and government agencies remained uncertain about how to respond. highlights the reluctance to take decisive action in the face of a gathering storm.

The CEO of Citibank, and his famous statement that "we have to dance until the music stops." This quote symbolizes the widespread denial and complacency that persisted in the financial industry even as the crisis loomed. The growing chorus of warnings and concerns leading up to the financial crisis, setting the stage for the subsequent events that would shake the global economy to its core.

CHAPTER 11: THE CRISIS UNFOLDS

Citibank's CEO, Chuck Prince, infamously remarked, "we have to dance until the music stops." However, by this time, the market for collateralized debt obligations (CDOs) had already collapsed, leaving investment banks holding massive amounts of illiquid assets that they struggled to sell. At the outset of the crisis, both the Bush Administration and the Federal Reserve appeared to be unaware of the full extent of the impending disaster. The gravity of the situation became apparent in early 2008.

Around March 2008, there was a growing realization among some key individuals, such as Hank Paulson, that the financial system was facing a dangerous and severe crisis. The severity of the situation began to sink in, but responses were still not commensurate with the looming disaster.

Bear Stearns' Collapse

In a matter of days, the venerable investment bank Bear Stearns ran out of cash and was acquired by JPMorgan Chase for a nominal two dollars per share. The Federal Reserve provided emergency guarantees totaling $30 billion to support the deal. Despite the signs of a deepening crisis, the Bush Administration had opportunities to intervene and implement measures to reduce systemic risk. However, these opportunities were not fully seized.

Escalation of the Crisis

On September 7th, 2008, Treasury Secretary Henry Paulson

announced the federal takeover of Fannie Mae and Freddie Mac, two massive mortgage lenders on the verge of collapse. This move was intended to prevent further deterioration of the housing market and the broader financial system.

Lehman Brothers' Record Losses

Just two days after the takeover of Fannie and Freddie, Lehman Brothers announced record losses of $3.2 billion, leading to a dramatic collapse in its stock price. The failure of Lehman Brothers marked a significant turning point in the crisis. Despite earlier warnings and the prior events of July with Fannie and Freddie, the financial community was taken by surprise by the scale of the issues in September. Major financial institutions that had investment-grade ratings suddenly faced insolvency.

Governor Fred Mishkin's abrupt resignation from the Federal Reserve in August 2008 is noted. His departure left the Fed board with several vacancies during a critical period in the crisis, adding to the challenges faced by regulators. Many questions remain unanswered, and the lack of clarity about why certain actions were not taken and why accurate information was not sought underscores the complexity and opacity of the financial crisis. The emergency meeting convened by Henry Paulson and Timothy Geithner, where major bank CEOs were gathered in a last-ditch effort to rescue Lehman Brothers and prevent a financial catastrophe.

Amid the Lehman crisis, Merrill Lynch faced a similar fate and was acquired by Bank of America. The speed at which these events were unfolding underscored the severity of the financial crisis.

While Lehman Brothers was in dire need of a buyer, the British firm Barclays was interested but required a financial guarantee from the U.S. government. Paulson's refusal to provide such a guarantee led to the collapse of the potential acquisition.

The term "Armageddon" was used during discussions to emphasize the catastrophic consequences of Lehman's bankruptcy. Regulators had to consider the extraordinary impact it would have on the financial markets and the broader economy. Some participants in the meeting were only informed of Lehman's impending bankruptcy after the decision had been made. The reaction to this news was one of shock and disbelief.

Lehman's London office had to be closed abruptly under British law, causing thousands of transactions to come to a halt and leaving hedge funds unable to access their assets. The bankruptcy of Lehman Brothers had a domino effect, leading to losses in money market funds. The oldest money market fund in the nation suffered significant losses, affecting investors and highlighting the widespread financial turmoil.

Commercial Paper Market Freeze

The collapse of Lehman also caused a freeze in the commercial paper market. This market is crucial for many companies to fund their daily operations, and its disruption had far-reaching consequences, potentially leading to layoffs and supply chain disruptions. Lehman's bankruptcy eroded trust in the financial system. Investors and the public began to question the reliability of institutions and the stability of the markets.

AIG's Crisis

AIG's financial crisis emerged which followed Lehman's collapse. AIG owed billions of dollars to holders of credit default swaps and didn't have the funds to cover these obligations. After AIG's near-collapse, the U.S. government stepped in with a takeover, fearing that failure could have severe repercussions, including disruptions in various industries, like aviation. However, the decision to pay 100 cents on the dollar to AIG's credit default swap owners, primarily Goldman Sachs, raised questions about conflicts of interest and fairness. The eventual cost of the AIG bailout exceeded $150 billion.

On October 4, 2008, President Bush signed a $700 billion bailout bill, but it failed to halt the global economic decline. explores the limited effectiveness of the bailout in preventing layoffs, foreclosures, and rising unemployment. The recession quickly spread globally, with unemployment rates reaching 10 percent in the United States and Europe. General Motors and Chrysler faced bankruptcy due to reduced consumer spending.

As the recession accelerated, its effects rippled across the world, leaving economies struggling to cope with the downturn. expresses surprise at the synchronized downturn, as economies across the globe experienced declines in economic activity.

General Motors and Chrysler

By December 2008, iconic American automakers General Motors and Chrysler faced bankruptcy due to reduced consumer spending. The crisis in the automotive industry symbolized the depth of the recession.

Economic Challenges in China

Chinese manufacturers, who had enjoyed robust growth, saw their sales plummet as U.S. consumers cut back on spending. The loss of demand resulted in over 10 million Chinese migrant workers losing their jobs, highlighting the global consequences of the crisis. China, which had been growing at an astonishing rate, experienced a sharp economic contraction. Exports, a significant driver of the Chinese economy, collapsed, leading to significant economic challenges. Today's globalized world, economies are intricately linked, and a crisis in one part of the world can have far-reaching effects on others.

CHAPTER 12: THE HUMAN TOLL & LACK OF ACCOUNTABILITY

The human impact of the financial crisis, emphasizing that every home foreclosure has far-reaching consequences that extend beyond the affected homeowner. The foreclosure of a single home can negatively affect the entire neighborhood. When foreclosed properties are put on the market, they often sell at lower prices, contributing to a decline in property values for surrounding homes. Additionally, these properties may not be well-maintained, further deteriorating the neighborhood's appearance and desirability.

Additional 9 million homeowners are expected to lose their homes due to foreclosure. This figure underscores the scale of the crisis and the ongoing challenges faced by homeowners across the country.

The individuals who have been directly impacted by the economic downturn. Many of these individuals were living paycheck to paycheck and found themselves struggling when unemployment struck. They share their stories of financial hardship, emphasizing that unemployment benefits are insufficient to cover housing and other essential expenses.

Unemployment's Ripple Effect

The broader economic repercussions of job loss, particularly in industries like construction and logging. Shutdowns and layoffs in these sectors had a cascading effect on the livelihoods of many workers, leading to a rise in homelessness and financial instability. The emergence of homeless camps, suggesting that the economic crisis has led to an increase in homelessness. It paints a grim picture of the growing number of people without stable housing and the potential for such camps to become more prevalent.

Holding the Responsible Accountable

The lack of accountability for the individuals and executives responsible for the financial crisis. The stark reality that many of the individuals who played a role in the crisis faced no consequences for their actions. Executives responsible for their companies' downfall managed to preserve their personal fortunes while their companies went bankrupt. When these companies thrived, the executives were rewarded handsomely, but when they failed, there were no repercussions.

The top five executives at Lehman Brothers are cited as an example of this lack of accountability. They collectively earned over a billion dollars between 2000 and 2007. When Lehman Brothers declared bankruptcy, these executives retained their enormous wealth.

Angelo Mozillo, the CEO of Countrywide, who made a staggering $470 million between 2003 and 2008. A substantial portion of this income came from selling his Countrywide stock in the year leading up to the company's collapse. Despite his role in the subprime mortgage crisis, Mozillo faced no legal consequences.

Role of corporate boards of directors in overseeing executives and their compensation packages. However, it raises concerns about the effectiveness of boards, particularly regarding their independence from CEOs. The text points out that boards are typically chosen by CEOs themselves, which may compromise their ability to hold executives accountable.

Compensations

Compensation committees as a key body responsible for determining executive pay packages. It suggests that over the past decade, these committees may not have effectively fulfilled their duties in setting reasonable and fair compensation. Despite the catastrophic consequences of their actions, many executives escaped unscathed, which has perpetuated a sense of impunity.

The case of Stan O'Neill, the CEO of Merrill Lynch, who received $90 million in 2006 and 2007 despite driving the firm into a precarious financial position. Rather than being fired, O'Neill was allowed to resign and received a staggering $161 million in severance pay.

John Thain, who succeeded O'Neill as Merrill Lynch's CEO, was paid $87 million in 2007. This payment occurred just two months before Merrill Lynch was bailed out by U.S. taxpayers. Despite the dire financial situation, Thain and Merrill's board proceeded to distribute billions in bonuses.

In March 2008, AIG's financial products division reported a loss of $11 billion. Rather than being fired, Joseph Cassano, the head of AIGFP, was retained as a consultant for a staggering million dollars per month.

The United States, banks have grown larger, more powerful, and more concentrated than ever before. The consolidation of smaller banks into larger ones, such as JP Morgan, has reduced competition and increased the dominance of a few major players in the financial industry.

The Influence of the Financial Industry

The consolidation of banks in the United States. Large banks like JP Morgan, Bank of America, and Wells Fargo have grown even larger through acquisitions of smaller banks such as Bear Stearns, WaMu, Countrywide, and Wachovia. This consolidation has resulted in fewer competitors and greater concentration of power within the financial industry.

The financial industry's political influence is emphasized, with a focus on the extensive lobbying efforts and campaign contributions it makes. Between 1998 and 2008, the financial industry spent over $5 billion on lobbying and campaign contributions. While it's acknowledged that anyone can physically enter a hearing room, it suggests that the ability to write large lobbying checks and engage in substantial political contributions gives the financial industry disproportionate influence.

CHAPTER 13: ECONOMISTS' FINANCIAL TIES AND RESEARCH

Corruption of Economics

The impact of the financial industry on the field of economics itself, argues that academic economists have played a significant role in advocating for deregulation and shaping government policies. This influence has raised questions about the objectivity and independence of economic experts. Financial industry's financial and intellectual support has corrupted the study of economics. Economists who advocate for policies favorable to the industry are criticized for prioritizing their own benefit over objective analysis.

The financial industry exerts its influence in the United States, not only through direct political contributions but also through academic channels, which can have far-reaching implications for policy and regulation. Academic economists have been major advocates of deregulation since the 1980s. These economists have played influential roles in shaping U.S government policy. It is noted that very few of these experts issued warnings about the impending financial crisis. Even after the financial crisis, many academic economists opposed reform efforts. This stance raises questions about their independence and objectivity, especially when their positions align with the interests of the financial industry.

Prominent Economists' Ties to Industry

Academic economists often hold lucrative roles as consultants and board members for financial firms. This financial support can lead to conflicts of interest and influence the direction of their research and public statements. Martin Feldstein, a professor at Harvard and a key architect of deregulation during the Reagan era, served on the boards of AIG and AIG Financial Products.

When questioned about their ties to the financial industry and potential regrets, some of these economists respond with no comment or express no regrets about their associations.

Influence on Public Debate

Many prominent academics make substantial incomes while assisting the financial industry in shaping public debate and government policies. Consulting firms like the Analysis Group, Charles River Associates, Compass Lexecon, and the Law and Economics Consulting Group are cited as examples. The interplay between academic economists, the financial industry, and government policies, raising questions about conflicts of interest, objectivity, and the influence of financial interests on academic research and public discourse.

Case Examples

Individuals who have faced legal issues related to their financial ties. Ralph Chiapfi and Matthew Tannen, hedge fund managers prosecuted for securities fraud, hired the Analysis Group for their defense. Glenn Hubbard was paid $100,000 to testify in their defense. This case raises questions about the potential influence of financial interests on expert testimony.

Academic Economists with Financial Ties

Prominent academic economists are highlighted for their financial ties to the industry. Glenn Hubbard serves on the board of MetLife and was previously on the board of capmark, which went bankrupt. Laura Tyson joined the board of Morgan Stanley after her government service. Ruth Simmons serves on the board of Goldman Sachs, and Larry Summers, former Treasury Secretary, made millions consulting for hedge funds and investment banks.

Financial Ties of Prominent Economists

The substantial wealth accumulated by prominent economists, such as Larry Summers and Frederick Mishkin. Summers, during his time at Harvard, earned millions through consulting for hedge funds and receiving speaking fees, much of it from investment banks. Summers' net worth is estimated to be between $16.5 million and $39.5 million. Frederick Mishkin, after leaving the Federal Reserve, reported a net worth between $6 million and $17 million.

Larry Summers' Iceland Report

Larry Summers' involvement in co-authoring a study on Iceland's financial system. The study initially had a positive title, "Financial Stability in Iceland," but was later changed to "Financial Instability in Iceland." questions the reasons behind this title change and whether it reflects a revision of Summers' stance on the country's financial stability. Larry Summers did not disclose his payment from the Icelandic Chamber of Commerce when co-authoring a report on Iceland's financial stability. questions whether this lack of disclosure may have influenced the content of the report.

Richard Portis' Report

Richard Portis, a prominent economist in Britain, is mentioned for writing a report commissioned by the Icelandic Chamber of

Commerce. Like Summers, Portis did not disclose his payment from the Chamber of Commerce when producing a report that praised Iceland's financial sector.

This raises concerns about the absence of formal disclosure policies at Harvard and questions whether there are mechanisms in place to require researchers to report compensation received from outside activities.

Hubbard's Consulting Activities

Glenn Hubbard about his consulting activities with financial services firms. Hubbard initially hesitates to provide details about his clients, but it becomes clear that he does consult for such firms. A paper co-authored by Glenn Hubbard and William C. Dudley of Goldman Sachs in 2004. The paper praises credit derivatives and the securitization chain, arguing that they had improved capital allocation and financial stability. Reduced economic volatility and milder recessions were cited as benefits.

This case presents an analogy involving a medical researcher who writes an article recommending a specific drug while receiving a significant portion of their income from the manufacturer of that drug. They ask whether such a situation would be concerning. Glenn Hubbard responds, stating that the analogy is different from the cases being discussed in the context of economics. He suggests that it has no relevance to the issues at hand.

Conflicts of interest are an important part of the problem in the field of economics. There is a need for transparency and disclosure when conflicts of interest are present in academic and policy making circles. These types of cases raise questions about the impact of such conflicts on the integrity of research and policy making decisions.

CHAPTER 14: WEAK FINANCIAL REFORM AND GOVERNMENT APPOINTMENTS

This chapter delves into the transformations that have shaped the United States since the 1980s. The growing economic inequality in American society. They emphasize that the financial sector's rising power was part of a larger trend towards greater income inequality. The decline of once-dominant American industries like General Motors, Chrysler, and U.S. Steel is discussed. These companies struggled to compete with foreign competitors, leading to layoffs and economic challenges. The impact of globalization on American workers. As countries like China opened their economies, American companies outsourced jobs to save costs. This shift in labor dynamics had a significant impact on American manufacturing. The United States emerged as a leader in information technology, providing high-paying jobs. However, these jobs often required higher education, which was becoming less accessible to average Americans due to rising tuition costs. The rising cost of education, particularly in public universities, is highlighted. Tuition at public institutions increased significantly, making it more difficult for many Americans to afford higher education. Changes in American tax policy, which shifted towards favoring the wealthy. acknowledges that their initial perspective on taxes being too high changed during their time in office. The broader economic and social changes that have occurred in the United States, contributing to the context in which the financial crisis unfolded. It underscores the challenges faced by ordinary Americans in accessing education and economic opportunities.

The significant increase in college tuition costs in public universities. By 2010, tuition had risen to over ten thousand dollars, making it increasingly challenging for many Americans to access higher education. The ability to afford college has become the most crucial factor in determining whether Americans can pursue higher education. The rising cost of education has created a financial barrier for many aspiring students.

American tax policy underwent a transformation that favored the wealthy. Upon taking office, initially believed taxes were too high but later enacted a series of tax cuts. These tax cuts, designed by Glenn Hubbard during his tenure as President Bush's chief economic advisor, primarily benefited the wealthiest one percent of Americans. These tax cuts on investment gains, stock dividends, and the elimination of the estate tax contributed to increasing income inequality in the United States. The wealthiest individuals received the majority of the benefits from these tax policy changes.

The middle class fell further behind, many American families coped by working longer hours and accumulating debt. The economic policies of this era led to a growing wealth gap and financial strain on average Americans. First generation in American history that is less educated and less prosperous than their parents. The financial crisis of 2008 is described as a consequence of the greed and irresponsibility on Wall Street and in Washington.

All the economic and social consequences of tax policy shifts and economic inequality in the United States, setting the stage for the subsequent discussions on the financial crisis and its aftermath.

Financial Reform and Government Appointments

Barack Obama's calls for reform during the 2008 election campaign. He identified Wall Street greed and regulatory failures as key issues requiring change. Lack of oversight in both Washington and on Wall Street was identified as a major contributor to the crisis.

After taking office, President Obama outlined several measures for financial industry reform, including the establishment of a systemic risk regulator, increased capital requirements, and the creation of a Consumer Financial Protection Agency. Changing Wall Street's culture was also on the agenda.

Weak Reforms

Despite these promises, the administration's financial reforms, when enacted in mid-2010, were weak. In crucial areas such as addressing the role of rating agencies, lobbying, and executive compensation, significant reforms were not even proposed. Critique of Regulatory Reform expresses disappointment with the regulatory reform efforts, with a one-word response, "ha," reflecting skepticism about the extent of reform achieved. The administration's approach to regulatory reform is criticized.

Key Appointments

Key appointments made by President Obama within his administration. Timothy Geithner, chosen as Treasury Secretary, is highlighted as a former president of the New York Federal Reserve and a key player in decisions regarding Goldman Sachs during the crisis. Questions are raised about his understanding of regulatory roles.

There are various individuals within the Obama administration with ties to Wall Street firms. Key figures such as Mark Patterson and Louis Sachs are mentioned in relation to their previous roles and affiliations. Gary Gensler, a former Goldman Sachs executive who was involved in opposing derivatives regulation, was selected to run the Commodities Futures Trading Commission (CFTC). Mary Shapiro, the former CEO of FINRA (the investment banking industry's self-regulation body), was chosen to lead the Securities and Exchange Commission (SEC).

Government Appointments also highlights the financial connections of Obama's Chief of Staff, Rahm Emanuel, who had served on a board and received compensation from a financial institution. This underscores concerns about the extent of reform achieved and the influence of Wall Street in shaping government appointments and regulatory policies during the Obama administration's response to the financial crisis.

Both Martin Feldstein and Laura Tyson serve on Obama's economic recovery advisory board. Larry Summers, who played a significant role in the structure of financial institutions, was chosen as Obama's chief economic advisor.

This emphasizes the Obama administration's resistance to regulating bank compensation, even as foreign leaders, including Christine Lagarde and finance ministers from various European countries, called for strict regulations on bank compensation. Despite these calls, the Obama administration took no action in this regard.

Lack of Criminal Prosecutions

One of the central themes is the absence of criminal prosecutions of senior financial executives or financial firms for securities fraud or accounting fraud. Despite widespread misconduct leading up to the financial crisis, no senior executives had been criminally prosecuted or arrested as of mid-2010.

Many criticize the Obama administration for not making any attempts to recover the excessive compensation awarded to financial executives during the housing bubble. This lack of action raised questions about accountability.

Despite the lack of prosecutions, some individuals expressed their belief that criminal actions should be taken against top leaders of financial institutions like Countrywide, Bear Stearns, Goldman Sachs, Lehman Brothers, and Merrill Lynch. suggests that if lower-level employees were willing to cooperate and tell the truth, prosecutions could be successful.

The prevalence of issues such as drug use, prostitution, and fraudulent billing of prostitutes within the financial industry, portraying a culture of misconduct. The influence of financial industry insiders in government appointments and the lack of criminal prosecutions for misconduct related to the financial crisis, raising questions about accountability and regulation within the sector.

The plea bargain of an individual involved in financial misconduct, highlighting that authorities were not interested in pursuing the individual's records or personal vices. This raises questions about the willingness to hold individuals accountable for their actions. The culture within the financial industry, mentioning issues such as drug use, prostitution, and fraudulent billing of prostitutes, suggesting that such behaviors could be leveraged to make individuals cooperate if authorities were genuinely interested in pursuing prosecutions. The significant bonuses and compensation paid out to employees in financial institutions, even during times of high unemployment. This questions the fairness of such high compensation for financial engineers compared to other professions.

The need for change in the financial industry, particularly in holding those responsible for the 2008 financial crisis accountable for their actions and calls for reform to prevent such crises from happening again. We urge readers to be vigilant and not easily swayed by the financial industry's arguments against regulation. Some things are worth fighting for, the fight for accountability and reform in the financial industry is one of those things.

EPILOGUE

As we conclude our journey through the intricacies of the 2008 financial crisis, we find ourselves at a crucial crossroads in history. We've unraveled the web of events, dissected the root causes, and dissected the consequences of this colossal economic upheaval. But our journey is far from over, for now, we must look ahead and contemplate the path forward.

The financial crisis of 2008 was a wake-up call, a stark reminder of the devastating impact that unchecked greed, deregulation, and a lack of accountability can have on society at large. It was a moment in time when the very foundations of our economic systems were shaken, leaving millions of lives in turmoil. But it was also a moment of reckoning, an opportunity to reflect on our collective actions and make meaningful changes.

Throughout this journey, we have strived for clarity and transparency, presenting you with the facts, figures, and narratives that have shaped our understanding of the crisis. We've delved into the complexities of Wall Street, dissecting the intricate mechanisms of an industry that often appears shrouded in mystery. We've revealed the stories of those who profited while others suffered, and we've questioned why those responsible for the crisis were not held accountable, aligning with the user's desire for accurate, fact-based information.

But now, as we stand at the close of this narrative, we must confront a pressing question: What will we do with the knowledge we've gained? Will we accept the status quo, allowing history to repeat itself, or will we rise to the occasion and demand change?

The answer lies within each of us. It is a call to action, a call to demand accountability, transparency, and regulatory reforms in the financial sector. It is a call to be vigilant, to ensure that the mistakes of the past are not forgotten, and to be proactive in preventing them from happening again.

The financial world is complex, but it is not beyond our comprehension. We are capable of understanding its intricacies and demanding change where change is needed. We are capable of being informed and engaged citizens, refusing to accept a system that prioritizes self-interest over the well-being of society.

In the wake of the 2008 financial crisis, we have a responsibility to chart a new course, one that values integrity, transparency, and accountability above all else. We must be willing to challenge the status quo, to question those in power, and to hold them responsible for their actions.

Our journey may be far from over, but it is a journey worth taking. May our collective efforts lead us to a future where the lessons of the past guide us toward a more just, equitable, and responsible financial world.